CLIQUES & CLONES

*Facing
Peer Pressure*

FRAN & JILL SCIACCA

ZondervanPublishingHouse
Grand Rapids, Michigan

A Division of HarperCollinsPublishers

Cliques & Clones
Facing Peer Pressure
Copyright © 1987, 1992 by Fran and Jill Sciacca
All rights reserved

[Previously published as *Cliques and Clones*
A Bible Study for Young Adults on Peer Pressure]

Requests for information should be addressed to:
Zondervan Publishing House
Grand Rapids, Michigan 49530

ISBN: 0-310-48031-0

Unless otherwise indicated, Scripture quotations are taken from *The Living Bible*, © 1971,
Tyndale House Publishers. Used by permission.

Scripture quotations marked NIV are taken from the HOLY BIBLE: NEW INTERNATIONAL
VERSION® (North American Edition). Copyright © 1973, 1978, 1984, by the International
Bible Society. Used by permission of Zondervan Publishing House.

"NIV" and "New International Version" are registered in the United States Patent and Trademark
Office by the International Bible Society.

All rights reserved. No part of this publication may be reproduced, stored in a retrieval
system, or transmitted in any form or by any means—electronic, mechanical, photocopy,
recording, or any other—except for brief quotations in printed reviews, without the prior
permission of the publisher.

Printed in the United States of America

92 93 94 95 96 / DP / 5 4 3 2 1

Why "Lifelines"?

Who in the world are Fran and Jill ... is it Sky-ocka??

The name "Sciacca" (actually pronounced "Shock-a") is probably not a familiar name to you. Let me take you on a quick trek through our lives so you will know who we are and why we care so much about you.

Fran grew up in the shadow of older identical twin brothers who were football stars. While their photos and accomplishments appeared regularly in newspapers and magazines, Fran found himself wondering who he was besides "the twins' little brother." In high school, he decided to take his talents "elsewhere," completely out of the arena of athletics; he set out to become the best bass guitarist he could be. His rock band was a success, and soon Fran also made it to the pages of the newspaper. On one occasion he played in front of 5,000 people at a "battle of the bands" in Milwaukee, Wisconsin. Fame became Fran's total focus in his search for "self." He was popular at school and was elected class president for three years.

In college, Fran quickly blazed his way to the top of his fraternity. The professional status of his new rock group also gave him personal pride. The band's popularity soared beyond the college campus, and Fran began doing "warm-up" for nationally known entertainers such as Chase and B. J. Thomas. He had finally "arrived" —or so he thought. But why, he wondered, was the feeling of emptiness still lodged so deep in his soul?

Then in one year's time the band began to break up, his girlfriend dumped him, and he received the devastating news that one of his brothers had been seriously wounded in the Vietnam War. It was as if someone had let the air out of his world. He felt alone in the universe. Even his 12 years of religious education in a private school didn't help him.

About this time, God brought a friend into Fran's life who had just committed his own life to Jesus Christ. Late one night in a quiet dorm room, Fran heard from him about the depth of God's love. For the first time, Fran had reason to believe that he was a valuable person, not because he was "cool," or a popular bass guitarist, but because the God of the universe loved him and had paid the penalty for his sin. Fran found the identity he had always longed for in the person of Jesus Christ.

Jill's Journey

I grew up in the "suburbs," graduating with a class of more than 700 students. My years in high school could best be characterized by my quest to know, "Where's the party?" But when I was alone, I often thought about life and death—even suicide. I wrote poems that exposed my inner fears but felt they were "safe" as simple assignments for English class. As best I could, I squelched my spiritual emptiness by dancing, partying, working a little, and playing a lot.

My folly and flippant approach to study in high school forced me to be on probation for the first quarter of college. I buckled down to get good grades but somehow managed to maintain my carefree lifestyle "to the max." I was dating a gifted art student, and together with other friends we embraced the sixties' counterculture. Our philosophy boasted that peace was possible; we could affect society and bring about lasting change. "We" were the answer to all of America's problems.

Yet in two years' time I witnessed the tragic folly of the sixties' philosophy in vivid detail: A best friend from high school had burned out on drugs. Another had died while on drugs. I had seen that our protests against the Vietnam War were leading to prison sentences. People were losing heart. Dropping out. My boyfriend had been committed to a psychiatric ward in a hospital. My best girlfriend, who had entered college on a scholarship, had quit, disillusioned with life. My rock star heroes had fallen from the thrones I'd placed them on. Jimi Hendrix had died. (I had been in the front rows at one of his concerts.) Jim Morrison was gone. Drugs and death seemed to go together. We were not the answer to America's woes—we were part of the problem!

So I fled from the fast lane and started studying philosophy, searching for answers but finding none. Finally, I desperately cried out to the God I had learned about in Sunday school as a child. I had always believed in him but never realized that I could know him personally. Committing my life to him, I made him my Lord and found the peace I hadn't found in all my searching. I joined the ranks of the revival on our college campus, the one that had also swept Fran into the faith. We were radical, but now we had an anchor and a purpose that was really destined to succeed.

And Then, Fran & Jill

We were married after graduation from college. Our first home was in Wisconsin, out in the country, where we attended a small church. There we immediately gravitated to the youth. Three years and one son later, the Lord led us to Denver, Colorado, where Fran went to seminary. While in Denver, we were again drawn to teens as Fran did field work at a local church. Two years and another son later, the Lord led us to Colorado Springs Christian School, where Fran has been teaching Bible in high school ever since! Now we also have the blessed bonus of twin daughters.

We need to tell you all of this for two reasons: First, everything that these studies deal with comes out of our own experience. Second, in many of the things that you're going to look at in *Lifelines: Bible Studies for Students*, we totally "blew it." So not only do we understand the issues at hand, we also know the pain and temptation that go with the territory.

We believe that a genuine relationship with Jesus Christ and with those who are committed to him is the most fulfilling and exciting thing on this sometimes perplexing planet! We're not talking about people who "play church." We're talking about those who are really serious about falling in love with and following the One who died for us.

So be assured that your struggles are familiar to us. They are foes that we have fought too. They are battles that we often lost. But we know there is a way of victory, and we want to help you discover that door of hope.

We pray that, through a personal study of God's Word, you will gain a new vision for a meaningful life, walking with the Lord and living in victory.

Fran and I are a "fun" team. He is the "architect"; I am the "builder." You will find the Bible study section of each chapter designed by Fran. I have helped Fran put a "personal touch" to the studies by telling a story you can relate to, about someone who has been a part of our lives. (Names, gender, and nonessential details have been altered to protect the privacy of those involved.)

There is one more thing we want you to know as you begin this Bible study—we really care about you!

What Is "Lifelines"?

Life is tough! Being a teenager is even tougher. You bounce somewhere between adulthood and childhood, ping-ponging back and forth, not really landing on either side, never really knowing which side you're supposed to be on at any given moment. The temptation to give in or give up may seem greater than you can bear. You probably feel as if you're sinking in a sea of pressures and problems too deep and wide to navigate. Let's face it, life's a battle. But ... on the other hand, is that so unusual?

What does it take to make the first-string soccer team? What's the cost of working your way to first-chair trumpet in the school band? How long did you have to practice to become the best guitarist at school? Remember those early-morning practices for the spring play? It seems as if everything significant has a price tag. Maybe that's the way it's supposed to be; maybe that's the way God planned it. But he also provides the help we need along the way. *Lifelines: Bible Studies for Students* is one of those helpers.

"Lifelines" Is Different

Lifelines: Bible Studies for Students is different. It won't help you "sail" through life, because nobody sails through life. But *Lifelines* will be honest with you about life, about God, about yourself, about your choices and your dreams. *Lifelines* promises "to put the cookies on the bottom shelf," to meet you right where you are and deal with the things that you have to deal with each day. It promises to provide answers where there are answers and to ask questions where they need to be asked.

But, just as in the rest of life, there are some costs that go with these Bible studies. What are they? Simply this: *Lifelines: Bible Studies for Students* promises to be honest with you, but you've got to be honest with yourself. And even more important—you've got to be honest with God. These studies are built on the presupposition that the Bible is God's Word. That means that your opinions and feelings have a genuine place in your life, but the final place is reserved for God's Word.

This Bible study cannot change your life; only God can do that. But, God can't guide a parked car. You're the one who's got to cooperate with God as you carefully work through this study.

You've got to be willing to let the Lord into your life, into your problems and pressures, into your battle. He wants to be beside you whether you are defeated or determined. If you are willing to pay this price, *Lifelines: Bible Studies for Students* could very well be one of the most exciting things that happens to you this year!

Things to Keep in Mind:

Here are some important thoughts to keep in mind as you begin:

#1 God is not a coach. He doesn't have a checklist for your performance. He loves you. In fact, he loves you just as you are as you begin this study.

#2 Apply what you learn to yourself. Resist the urge to think of others who "really need to hear" what you are learning.

#3 Be faithful. Whatever your commitment is, whether to a group or simply to yourself, keep it. Make it your goal to finish the study.

#4 Be realistic. Weeds grow quickly, but an oak tree takes time. Look for small ways to grow. If you set goals that are too tough, you'll become discouraged. Small victories will encourage you to keep going.

Lifelines: Bible Studies for Students accepts the fact that much of life is a battle for you. But, you can win.

> You've got to know there's a bigger plan.
> Room to fall, room to stand.
> Pray for the plan to begin in you.
> Keep your heart true!*

> [sung by Amy Grant]

God wants you to win the battle, but remember: You can't have a victory where there's been no fight. You may fall—we all do—but learn to stand!

*"Who to Listen To" by Gary Chapman, Tim Marsh, and Mark Wright.
© 1985 Blackwood Music, Inc./Land of Music/Riverstone Music, Inc.
All rights reserved. International copyright secured. Used by permission.

How to Use This Bible Study

This Bible study is part of a series entitled *Lifelines: Bible Studies for Students*. Each study in the series centers around a single issue that you, as a teenager, face in the twentieth century. This study, *Cliques & Clones,* deals with the subject of peer pressure.

Each chapter of *Cliques & Clones* includes a real-life story, some personal study questions, and a summary discussion. Look for one major truth, a "Lifeline," as you go through each chapter. If there are specific things the study asks you to do, be sure to do them. The personal insights you pull out of these pages won't help you until you begin to put them into practice.

The only things you will need to complete this study are a Bible, a pen, and an open heart. We suggest that you use the *New International Version* or *The Living Bible*. Make sure that your Bible has both the Old and the New Testaments. We suggest you also have a spiral notebook to record thoughts and ideas that come to you while you study.

If you study *Cliques & Clones* in a group, you'll find the optional group discussion questions in each chapter's "Bottom Line" section enlightening and helpful.

There is another optional section near the end of each chapter, entitled "His Lines." These are two passages from the Bible that might be helpful as you seek to make the "Lifeline" from that chapter a reality in your own life. You can memorize these verses, put them on your mirror, in your locker, or on the dashboard of your car. Plant them anyplace where they can prompt you to remember the truth when you need it the most.

Other Lifelines

If you enjoy *Cliques & Clones*, you may want to try these other *Lifelines* studies:

Are Families Forever?
Strengthening Family Ties

Burgers, Fries & a Friend to Go
Making Friends

Does Anyone Else Feel This Way?
Conquering Loneliness and Depression

Good News for a Bad News World
Understanding the Gospel

Is This the Real Thing?
What Love Is and Isn't

So What's Wrong with a Big Nose?
Building Self-Esteem

What Really Matters?
Setting Priorities

1

Who's Pushing Me?

Opening Lines

I was determined never to do drugs. I would drink, but drugs were for people who had copped out on life, people who had no plans. Not me! I cared, I had plans—at least, plans to finish high school.

But there I sat, a sophisticated senior from a small blue-collar town in Wisconsin, at a party in an upper-class Minneapolis suburb. A friend and I were staying with my uncle for a week. My brother had slipped me the phone number of the younger sister of a girl he had dated and suggested we give her a call. I called, and she invited us to a party. "My parents are out of town," she said. "It's going to be a blast!" Without too much hesitation, we went.

When Bill and I arrived, I'll never forget how intrigued and impressed I was by all the sports cars parked on the pavement. Once inside, I was even more mystified. I'd never seen such clothes-conscious, cool-looking high school students in my life! The girls were all "awesome," and the guys were good-looking too. It was almost as if I'd found myself among the pages of a high fashion catalog.

As the party progressed, so did the drinking, including my own. I stumbled into a room filled with bodies and blue smoke. It suddenly hit me that they were all getting high! No sooner had this realization rooted itself, when Bill handed me a joint and said, "C'mon, Fran, go ahead; this stuff is incredible!" Everyone in the room was suddenly looking at me. All the sophisticated, summer-bronzed faces came into focus, and they were staring, waiting to see if I was "cool." I sat down and, needless to say, was initiated into the world of drugs that evening.

But, what could I have done? Those kids were all rich, good-looking, and seemingly successful. I cared about their approval and acceptance. Saying "no" was out of the question, wasn't it? I mean, they would have thought I was a nerd! I didn't really have any options—did I?

On the Lines

1. Look at 1 Samuel 15: 1–9. What was the assignment God gave to King Saul (verses 1–3)?

_____

_____

What did Saul do (verses 4–9)? _____

_____

Why do you think Saul did what he did? _____

_____

_____

Now look at 1 Samuel 15:24. Saul explains his actions. What is his own explanation?

_____

_____

_____

What do you think Saul meant by "afraid"? What was he afraid of?

_____

_____

2. Turn to Galatians 2:11–13. In this passage Paul wrote about Peter, who at the time was the leader of all the Christians. What did Peter do that upset Paul (Note: another name for some of the Jews who became Christians was "the circumcision party." Also, a Jew would *never* eat with a Gentile, someone who was not a Jew.)

_____

_____

What does Paul say caused Peter to do what he did (verse 12)?

_____

3. Turn to Proverbs 29:25. What comes to your mind when you think of a snare or trap?

_____

_____

How do you see the truth of this verse in Saul's and Peter's lives?

_____

_____

Do you see this truth in your own life? Explain. _____

_____

_____

4. Thinking back to what happened to me at my party, and what happened to Saul and Peter, where would you say the pressure came from for us to do what we did? Was it from outside us or inside us? Explain.

_____

_____

_____

Between the Lines

1. Make a list of the things that you would never give away, to anyone (think hard on this one).

_____

_____

_____

Look over your list. Did you have "my freedom" or "my individuality" on the list? Why not?

_____

_____

_____

2. Tomorrow, I want you to make one radical venture. I want you to speak your mind in one of your classes where you've never been noticed before, because you've been quiet and reserved. Or, pull a person aside whom you've been wanting to talk to but couldn't because of fear. Risk being different simply because you're in charge! Do you dare to wear something outrageously different? Perhaps something you've wanted to put on, but wouldn't because you pondered with fear the opinions of your peers.

Closing Lines

Peer pressure has been defined by someone as "that hungry urge to conform to the standards of others without any conscious or reasonable personal decision to do so." You simply find yourself performing in a certain way to please the significant people in your life. Saul did it, and so did Peter. Do you? God's Word calls peer pressure "the fear of man." Fear is an inner response; it is my reaction to certain circumstances. In the same way, peer pressure is not "out there," it's inside you. Only you really make the decisions about whom you will allow to be your influential peers, and to what degree they will make demands on you. Not only do you conform to please them, they also control you. Is this what you want?

If you are willing to stand on your own two feet for what you really want for yourself, you will soon discover that genuine joy comes from not being a clone. I did not become famous to my party peers in Minneapolis. I simply conformed to their standards on how to be "cool" and consequently destroyed my own desire never to do drugs.

Lifeline:

Peer pressure comes from inside me.

His Lines

Proverbs 29:25

1 Samuel 15:24

The Bottom Line (For Group Discussion)

1. Have your group listen to "Not Gonna Bow" sung by Russ Taff on his *Medals* album. Discuss how the song touches on the subjects covered in this chapter.

2. Discuss as a group what unique peer pressures you feel that are a result of being a Christian.

3. Have six members (or less) of your group dress up in their "Sunday best." Take a picnic basket with their parents' best silver, china place settings, goblets, a white tablecloth, and candles. Then go to McDonald's for lunch!! Have them report back to the rest of the group about what it was like, what pressures they felt, if they had fun (why or why not).

2

When the Party's Over

Opening Lines

Brenda was a blast! She's one of those rare people whose laugh is as contagious as the flu. I remember many nights when we literally held our sides in pain as we fell to the floor in hysterics. That was almost twenty years ago. Brenda still has some hurts, but they're no longer from laughing.

She was fresh out of high school when she fell in love. The attention this young man gave her filled the crater created by her father's frequent criticism of her and his lack of affection. Her boyfriend's influence in her life was significant. Their involvement deepened, as did her dependence on him for self worth. As is often the case in a relationship like this, she loosened her moral standards until finally her greatest fear became a reality—she was pregnant!

Her father had repeatedly told her as a young girl that if she ever got pregnant outside of marriage, she would disgrace him. Her boyfriend didn't want the baby either. He offered to pay for her to go to Mexico and have an abortion (it was illegal in the U.S. at that time). Caught in the conflict of placating a father she couldn't please and losing a boyfriend she couldn't live without, she went to Mexico—alone. After all, her boyfriend loved her, didn't he? She'd be spending the rest of her life with him, wouldn't she? And even if it was wrong to have an abortion right now, she had the rest of her life ahead of her. Right?

On the Lines

1. Pick one word from the list below that you think best defines what it means to be deceived.

☐ confused   ☐ tricked   ☐ misinformed
☐ misled   ☐ cheated

Why did you pick this particular word instead of the others?

_____

_____

2. In Galatians 6:7,8, Paul talks about one issue we can be deceived about, laying down a principle about how the choices we make affect our lives. What do you think he means by the phrase, "sows to please his sinful nature"?

_____

_____

_____

What do you think he means by "sows to please the Spirit"?

_____

_____

3. Paul also says that both of these types of people will "reap." That is, there will be results or consequences from choices. Think very carefully about this idea of "sowing" and "reaping." When you plant seeds in a garden, can you tell what's been planted right after they have been planted? Explain.

_____

_____

_____

Can you harvest your crop a week after it's planted? Explain.

_____

_____

4. Look back over your answers to questions 2 and 3. What truth do you see here about when we actually experience the consequences (reap) from what we do (sow)?

_____

_____

_____

5. Look back to question 1. How could a person be deceived about what you said in your answer to question 4?

_____

_____

_____

6. How many of the friends you have right now do you honestly think will be your friends ten years from now?

_____

7. According to what you've discovered about choices and consequences in this chapter, which do you think lasts longer: your friendships, or the consequences of choices you made because of your friendships? Explain.

_____

_____

_____

8. Summarize one new discovery you've made about peer pressure as a result of this chapter.

_____

_____

_____

Between the Lines

1. Who are your two peers who influence your decisions the most? Write down their names. Now, ask two adults which of their high school friends influenced them the most. Then ask if they are still friends with them today. Also, ask them how being friends with these people affected the lives they are living today.

_____

_____

2. Take about thirty minutes by yourself to do this. Write down what "seeds" you are sowing in your own life right now. You can do this by reviewing your activities for the past month and listing them in the left column below. Then, list in the center column the people who have been with you during these activities. Finally, in the right column, write down what you think could be possible "harvests" in your life as a result of these activities. (For example, how they might affect your health, marriage, values or parenting) You may need to discuss the possible "harvest" with an adult (teacher, youth pastor, etc.) who you know has been there.

SEEDS	PEOPLE	HARVEST

Now, cross off all the names of your friends from the list—because they will probably not be your close friends ten years from now. Next cross off all the activities, because they will be history ten years from now. You are now left all alone with the "harvests." Looking realistically at what is on this list, are there some "seeds" in your life that you feel you need to stop sowing right now? What do you need to do to stop sowing them? (Note: If this list contains very personal information, you might want to destroy it after this exercise.)

Closing Lines

My friend Brenda never married her boyfriend. In fact, she has totally lost touch with him. Since her abortion, she has committed her life to Christ, married a loving Christian man and has four beautiful children.

If you were to ask my friend if she is happy she would say without hesitation, "Yes!" But she would also admit with sadness that she has a scar that has stayed with her which reminds her of the wrong choices she made many years ago. By God's grace, the pain is gone, but the scar still stands as a witness that there was a time of sowing bad seed in her life, a season she will never totally forget.

The friendships you have now will not last forever. In fact, many will not last past high school. But, the choices you make because of those friendships will produce effects in your life that will go on past graduation. Just as it takes time for seeds sown to produce a harvest, so, too, the choices you make today will produce results in your future even if you don't see any effect yet. This is just as true for the right choices as it is for wrong choices. One of the hardest yet most critical truths you need to embrace is that your present friends possibly will not be around when the harvest happens in your life, even though you were together when the choices were made.

Lifeline:

The consequences of my choices will outlast my friendships.

His Lines

Galatians 6:7

1 Timothy 4:8

The Bottom Line (For Group Discussion)

1. Have the members of your group spend an evening with one of their parents looking through their parent's yearbook from high school (if they have one). Have them talk about the concepts of sowing and reaping. Ask them to tell you what has happened to friends of theirs who made right choices and those who made wrong choices. When the group meets, discuss what happened.

2. Why is it so much harder to make choices for the future than it is for the present?

3. What do you think are some of the most dangerous bad choices you can make? Why?

4. What do you think are some of the most beneficial good choices you can make? Why?

3

It's Your Choice

Opening Lines

Janet never communicated in class all year. I was naturally very surprised when she stopped me after class one day and said she wanted to talk. My last hour was free, so we agreed to meet at my "office," a large black couch in the upstairs lobby.

Her story was a sad one, and painful to ponder. I couldn't imagine what it was like to actually experience it. Her parents were planning to divorce in the next three months, supposedly to end a messed-up marriage. Janet's father consistently called her names that maligned her moral purity. He tried to listen in on her telephone conversations, and interrogated her thoroughly after each date. As she poured out this narration of distrust and shame from her father, I couldn't help but notice her countenance. It told a tale of its own. The softness that normally characterizes a 15-year-old girl's face vanished. Her eyes didn't sparkle and dance, and wrinkles were developing in the corners. She sought to hide them with heavy make-up. It was a face that bore the imprint of impurity, or hurt, or both.

As we talked further, I discovered that all of Janet's male

"friends" were well out of high school. She and another girl from church were hanging around with some guys who had full-time jobs and their own apartments. I'm sure the image of independence these young men were flaunting stood as an appealing alternative to the oppression and restrictions Janet felt in her own home. It was also obvious, at least to me, that Janet felt tremendous pressure to act older when she was with these young men. And in this case, that meant having a more "adult attitude" about premarital sex, drugs, and dating. Janet's peers at school, as a rule, didn't engage in or approve of the things she was doing. If she had chosen to develop friendships with girls and guys her own age, she might have experienced a different pressure—pressure to stay pure and freedom to be a teenager rather than an adult. Though Janet felt free, she was actually in bondage. She was trapped in a teenaged body, trying to act like an adult. She was fighting her father, but she was also engaged in a battle with herself and God's design for her physical and emotional development.

I met with Janet three or four more times. I counseled her to consider breaking off her relationships with these older guys and to develop some closeness with her classmates. I even suggested a few names of students I thought she'd find fellowship and security with. She told me, "You don't really understand." She believed these guys really cared about her; they accepted her.

Janet chose to stay with her old friends. She came to me only two more times—once to talk about her involvement with cocaine, and the other because she thought she might be pregnant. After that, she quit coming to see me.

Is who I choose for friends really that important? Can my comrades actually keep me out of sin and trouble as well as pull me into it? I can be my own person no matter whom I hang around with, can't I?

On the Lines

1. One of the most powerful verses in the Bible on the issue of peer influence is Proverbs 13:20. Look it up in your Bible. What comes to your mind when you think of a wise person?

_____

_____

What comes to your mind when you think of a fool?

_____

_____

_____

According to this verse, who is affected most by these relationships?

_____

2. Do you know what characterizes a wise person? Look up the following verses and write out the characteristics of a wise person described in the verse:

Job 28:28 _____

Prov. 12:15 _____

Prov. 12:18 _____

Matthew 7:24 _____

2 Tim. 3:15 _____

What characterizes a "fool"?

Psalm 53:1 _____

Prov. 15:5 _____

Prov. 18:2 _____

Prov. 20:3 _____

Prov. 26:11 _____

Prov. 28:26 _____

3. These verses seem to teach that there is such a thing as positive peer pressure as well as negative peer pressure. Using your answers from question 2, write out what you understand the Bible to be saying about each.

Positive peer pressure: _____

_____

_____

_____

Negative peer pressure:

_____

_____

_____

_____

4. Summarize any new discovery you have made about peer pressure from this chapter.

_____

_____

_____

Between the Lines

1. In the space below, write the initials of your four best friends (those you spend the most time with) under the heading "Companions." Then look back over your answers to question 2 above. For each of these four friends, circle the "F" if that friend exhibits more characteristics of a fool than a wise person. Circle a "W" if the opposite is true.

COMPANIONS
_____

1.   F   W

2.   F   W

3.   F   W

4.   F   W

Now, look again at your answers. Are these four friendships going to make you grow wise or suffer harm? Do you need to strengthen or break off any of them? Remember Proverbs 13:20.

2. Hebrews 13:7 talks about imitating the faith of older Christians whose lives are solid. Is there an older Christian who you admire? Why not call him or her and see if you could spend an afternoon together. Perhaps you could help that person with some chore around the house, and talk as you work. Talk about your weaknesses. Ask for help.

3. Is there someone you know who is hanging around with the wrong crowd simply because the good kids wouldn't let him or her into their circle? What can you do to be a positive peer to that person?

Closing Lines

Janet's conclusion that I didn't understand wasn't true. My wife, Jill, faced a decision like Janet's in her high school days. Though she once painfully chose not to hang around with a peer group that was affecting her in a negative way, she now is grateful as she looks back and sees her former friends' lives terribly tarnished by the sin that began in high school. And Jill did find many new friends.

Peer pressure isn't always bad. There's such a thing as positive peer pressure, which I experience when I am around "wise" friends. I am the one who suffers from negative relationships, but I am also the one who benefits from positive peers. The whole thing seems to hinge on whom I choose as friends. Amy Grant is totally right when she sings:

> You've got to know who to
> Who not to listen to.
> You've got to know who to
> Who not to listen to.
> They're gonna hit you from all sides
> Better make up your mind
> Who to, who not to listen to.*

Whom are you listening to??

Lifeline:

The friends I choose will affect who I am.

His Lines

Proverbs 13:20

1 Corinthians 15:33

The Bottom Line (For Group Discussion)

1. How can we drive people away from us and into the wrong crowd? Is this serious? Why?

*"Who to Listen To" by Gary Chapman, Tim Marsh and Mark Wright. © 1985 Blackwood Music, Inc./Land of Music/Riverstone Music, Inc. All rights reserved. International Copyright secured. Used by permission.

2. Have you ever experienced positive peer pressure? Explain.

3. Listen to "Who to Listen To" sung by Amy Grant. Discuss how it relates to this chapter. (The song is on her *Unguarded* album.)

4. Have each group member share who his or her hero is, and why. Then ask each of them to decide whether that person is a positive or negative hero.

5. What would a Christian hero be like? Describe him or her.

4

Why Won't God Help Me?

Opening Lines

"The back seat of a car is no place to think first about what your moral standards are." The room was strangely silent as my students pondered this truth that many had never thought through before.

I had asked Scott, a close friend of ours, to do a seminar on dating during an interim week for some 10th–12th graders at our school. He is one of those insightful individuals who can quickly capture an audience; and he had certainly struck a sensitive nerve in the thirty students who turned out for this seminar.

The point Scott had just made triggered for me a multitude of recollections of the many students who had previously talked to me that year. They were frustrated because they felt as if God had abandoned them when they needed him the most. A common question was, "How could God let this happen?" They had prayed meaningfully in the midst of a potentially sinful situation, and God hadn't come through. They had found themselves in frustrating circumstances where the pressure to do something wrong was overwhelming. But when they cried out in their hearts that God would not let them do it, he wouldn't bail them out. Some had sought God before they were actually swept into the situation, but that didn't seem to work either. Didn't God care? Isn't he powerful enough to keep me from giving in? Why didn't he help me? We're supposed to pray in situations like this, aren't we?

On the Lines

One of the most fascinating stories about coping with peer pressure is found in Genesis 39. It is the story of Joseph, who was hated by his brothers and sold into slavery. Eventually he became a famous leader in Egypt. Read Genesis 39:1–12.

1. What pressure was Joseph facing? (verses 6,7) _____

_____

_____

2. What evidence is there in verse 10 that this pressure was intense?

_____

3. How do you think Joseph was feeling? Why? (Think hard on this one.)

_____

_____

_____

4. How did he respond to this pressure (verses 8,10)? (Hint: he had two responses.)

_____

_____

_____

5. To what extent did Joseph go in his attempt to avoid temptation (verse 10)?

_____

_____

6. Look at verses 8 and 9. Mark one phrase below that you think best explains why Joseph didn't give in to this pressure:

☐ it was improper   ☐ he would have gotten caught

☐ he could have lost his important job   ☐ he didn't want to

☐ it was wrong   ☐ it was a sin against God

Explain your choice. Use information from the verses to support your answer.

_____

_____

_____

Do you think Joseph had to stop and think about what he was going to do in this situation? Why or why not?

_____

_____

Do you think Joseph made his choice about what to do on the spot, or do you think he had actually made up his mind long before this pressure situation occurred? Explain.

_____

_____

Do you think it would have been a good idea for Joseph to go back home and pray something like, "God, I am going back into her bedroom tomorrow just to explain how I feel. Please protect me."? Why or why not?

_____

_____

_____

Let's suppose he went back, sincerely attempting to be honest with her, and she began to seduce him again. As they sat down on the couch, Joseph prayed, "Lord, keep me strong." Does that seem like a fair prayer for God to answer? Explain.

_____

_____

2. Have you ever thought about certain things that you will not do under any circumstances? What are they?

_____

_____

What are the places or circumstances where these standards of yours could possibly be broken the easiest?

_____

_____

_____

3. Looking back over this study, do you think it's better to ask God to give you strength in the midst of a pressure situation, or to avoid the situation altogether? Use Joseph as an example in your explanation.

_____

_____

_____

4. What about the occasional instances when you are innocently thrust into a situation where sin stalks you. How can you escape?

_____

_____

Between the Lines

1. Establish a list of "unshakable unbreakables," specific things that you will not do, anywhere, under any circumstances. They could be moral standards or activities in general that you believe are wrong for you as a Christian.

My "Unshakable Unbreakables"

_____   _____

_____   _____

_____   _____

2. Establish a personal set of "No Trespassing Zones," specific places or situations where you will not go under any circumstances (for example, a party where the parents are out of town).

My Personal No Trespassing Zones

_____   _____

_____   _____

_____   _____

Closing Lines

The truth is, being in the midst of a situation is the worst time and place to try to establish a moral standard for your life. I recall a sophomore girl whom I had grown close to because of our many conversations. She had asked to talk with me one day over lunch. She was getting increasingly physically involved with her boyfriend. Her boyfriend was putting enormous pressure on her. As she related the story to me, I sensed the seriousness of her situation. She did not. As sensitively and compassionately as I could, I suggested that she either break off the relationship, or at least not allow herself to be alone with him for long periods of time. She was opposed to my counsel and asked why she should follow this advice. I warned her, "Because if you don't, I'm afraid you could be pregnant before the year is out." She stared at me, her face aroused with anger, and insisted, "I would never do that! Besides, the Lord would never let that happen either!" She stood up and stormed out of the room. I had cared enough to be candid, and it cost me a good friendship. Sadder still is that she had three pregnancy tests before the school year was out!

It is essential that you establish the "Unshakable Unbreakables" for your life, the limits that you *will not break*. And then, mark your "No Trespassing Zones," the places and situations you will not go. I can tell you from my own failures and those of many students I have counseled, that the "No Trespassing Zones" are almost more critical than the "Unshakable Unbreakables." We are a weak people, and even our earnest intentions can collapse under certain circumstances. Many casualties who have crumbled in temptation will tell you that a wall of good intentions will give way unless the wall is unshakably and unbreakably established deep in granite.

Lifeline:

I need "No Trespassing Zones" for my life.

His Lines

Proverbs 4:26

Proverbs 15:24

The Bottom Line (For Group Discussion)

1. What are some ways your group can help members maintain their "Unshakable Unbreakables" and "No Trespassing Zones"?

2. Discuss what God would actually have to do to deliver us from the midst of a pressure situation that we put ourselves in. Use your imagination. How would he do it? Is this realistic?

3. What happens if you totally blow it in this area? Does God forgive? What does he want me to do at this point? How do I pick up the pieces?

5

Surprise!

Opening Lines

Jill was at a friend's house along with a few other eighth grade girls. She wasn't where her parents thought she would be, but "no big deal," she figured; they were having wholesome fun! As they sat listening to some records and drinking soda, they heard a car honk in the driveway. One of the girls parted the curtains and called out, "Hey, it's Jim, and he's driving a really cool car!" The girls all filed out of the house and dashed up to the driver's window. "Where did you get the car?" they all asked at once. "I stole it," Jim said smiling. "Hop in; let's take it for a spin!"

One after another, the girls crawled into the stolen car. A group of grade school girls and several guys, all laughing and shouting their way to what is correctly called at police headquarters, "Grand Theft—Auto"! Jill sat in the car along with her friends, the result of a split-second decision. Her conscience condemned her actions, but she determined to ignore it as no one else seemed to feel guilty or concerned about the consequences if they were to get caught. If someone had told Jill that morning that she would end up in a stolen car later that evening, and had given her three hours to think it over, she wouldn't even have gone to the friend's house. Oh, it's true that if she had obeyed her parents in the first place she wouldn't have ended up in such a mess. But, she did disobey, and she did end up in the stolen car. And she did violate her conscience that prompted her to pull out.

The last thing Jill was thinking about when she went over to her friend's house is that she would be an accomplice in grand theft—auto! If you were to ask her, she would tell you, "I wasn't expecting it. It kinda came out of nowhere!"

How do you handle peer pressure situations that "come out of nowhere"? What were Jill's options? Did she really have any? It would have been out of the question to stand alone in the driveway and watch all her friends drive off. Right?

On the Lines

1. Matthew 26 contains the story of Jesus' last meal with his twelve closest friends just before he was crucified. During the meal, Jesus predicted that when he was captured, they would all desert him. Look at Peter's response to Jesus' prediction (Matthew 26:31–33, 35).

How did Peter feel about his own commitment to what he believed (this was one of his "unshakable unbreakables"!)?

_____

_____

In all fairness to Peter, I think he really believed what he said about himself. Do you? Explain.

_____

_____

_____

Now, read John 18:1–3. This is the capture Jesus predicted earlier. If you had been there with Jesus, how would you have felt? Why?

_____

_____

Look at verse 10 of John 18. Do you see any evidence in this verse
that Peter's statement in Matthew 26:35 was true?

_____

_____

2. After Jesus was arrested, he was taken to the high priest for his
first trial. Peter followed him. Peter had just stood up to a whole
bunch of armed soldiers and the religious leaders of his day. He
stood faithful to Jesus. Look at John 18:15–18, 25–27. How did
Peter handle this situation?

_____

_____

_____

Which of the following do you think best explains why Peter stood
tall before the guards but fell apart with the little girl?

☐ The guards were less threatening than the little girl.

☐ Peter's friends were all watching with the guards, but
he was alone with the little girl.

☐ Peter acted in fear with the guards.

☐ The little girl caught Peter totally off guard. He was not
expecting her question.

Explain why you picked the answer that you did. _____

_____

3. I believe this story of Peter has an important truth about peer
pressure: Often the toughest peer pressure situations arrive completely unannounced. How does a person deal with a surprise

situation like this? It will happen to you, even though you feel that you've got your "unshakable unbreakables" and your "no trespassing zones" nailed down tight! You will find yourself in situations that you haven't anticipated. There are two important ways to deal with surprise pressure situations:

PRINCIPLE #1
Look at Proverbs 13:3 and James 1:19. Now look back at Peter in John 18:15–18. In light of what the verses in Proverbs and James teach, what could Peter have done instead?

_____

_____

_____

Write out one possible way from the above verses of handling surprise peer pressure.

_____

_____

_____

PRINCIPLE #2
Look at 2 Timothy 2:22 and Genesis 39:11,12. From these two verses, write out a second possible way of handling surprise peer pressure.

_____

_____

_____

4. Summarize any new discoveries you have made about peer pressure from this chapter.

_____

_____

_____

Between the Lines

1. Do you think you have the courage to leave a surprise peer pressure situation? Write out what *you* would do in each of the following situations. Be honest!

A dozen or so friends from your school or church youth group are having a popcorn and movie bash. One of the parents has rented three movies for the evening. The movies are all pretty clean. After you arrive, you discover that one of the kids has secured several "R" rated movies. The plan is to watch the "R" rated movies and switch back to the movies the parents rented whenever they are starting to come down into the basement where your party is. Most of your friends seem to think this is a fine idea.

I would _____

_____

_____

You're on a double date with your best friend. After they pick you up, one of the guys pulls out some pot, lights up, and starts passing it around.

I would _____

_____

_____

_____

You are invited to an overnight at a friend's house. Your friend's parents are home, and everything looks fine. After you go to bed, your friend tells you that he has invited two girls from your class over "just to talk." They're going to sneak in the basement window in your friend's bedroom around midnight.

I would _____

_____

_____

Closing Lines

Often the toughest peer pressure situations attack us as surprises. If you knew they were coming, you could more easily deal with them and distance yourself. Probably the best response you can have is to get out! If you were trapped in a burning house or on a sinking boat, chances are you would make every effort to climb out as quickly as you could. Sometimes, quickly pulling out of a surprise peer pressure situation can be a way of "saving your life."

Another possible response is to think before you speak. If Peter hadn't "shot off his mouth" when that little girl provoked him with her penetrating question, he might not have ended up publicly denying Jesus.

The bottom line here is simply that you will face peer pressure situations you haven't planned on. Your first reaction will usually determine what ultimately happens.

Lifeline:

Running away is sometimes the best way to fight peer pressure.

His Lines

2 Timothy 2:22

Psalm 1:1

The Bottom Line (For Group Discussion)

1. Share answers to question 1 of "Between the Lines."

2. Would the members in the group ever be willing to help someone who wanted to get out of a surprise peer pressure predicament? What would they be willing to do?

3. Do you have a responsibility to expose parties and activities that are wrong? Explain your answer.

4. Discuss surprise situations you have faced and get the group to talk about what you could have done.

6

Standing Alone

Opening Lines

My hometown was small—*real* small. But I went to a private high school in a larger city seventeen miles away. I always felt like some sort of alien; I didn't really "belong" in either town. I spent my school time in a spot where I didn't live, and spent my leisure hours in a town where my classmates didn't live! The result was that I had a very, very difficult time making friends. I constantly felt as if I was trying to break into groups of kids who lived in another city. It was tough! Being accepted and liked was probably more important to me than to my classmates, because for me it was so much harder to achieve.

One Friday night, I was walking all alone on a street in the city where I went to school. Suddenly, a carload of guys from another school pulled up and shouted, "Hey, Sciacca, we're going to Point (a nearby town) to get drunk. C'mon along!" Most of them were popular wrestlers from the large public high school. A few guys from my own school had introduced me to them at a dance or a party. I recognized them, but I couldn't remember from where. The invitation was appealing. Going drinking with a carload of cool wrestlers seemed like a dream come true in my non-Christian mind. But I turned to them and blurted, "No thanks." "Aw c'mon, Sciacca," they beckoned, "we're gonna have a blast!" For some reason I refused again, and they drove off sputtering something about whether or not I was a real man, and other encouraging statements!

I remember strolling down the sidewalk that night—alone. I thought I'd blown the one big chance to break into one of the top groups. Had I really blown it? Was it really worth it? I knew drinking under age was wrong, but this might have cost me the recognition I so desperately coveted. Having friends in high school is what it's all about. Right?

On the Lines

1. Let's go back to our friend Joseph. In the last chapter we saw him running out the door from a woman who was begging him to go to bed with her (Genesis 39:6–12). What was the outcome of Joseph's choice (Genesis 39:13–20)?

_____

_____

Considering what happened to him, do you think Joseph's decision to run was worth it? Explain.

_____

_____

Look hard at the passage in Genesis 39. What did Joseph lose and what did he gain by refusing to yield to the pressure?

His Losses	His Gains

2. What do you think you could lose if you refused to give in to the peer pressure you face? List your losses in order of importance to you (#1 = most important, etc.) Be honest!

MY LOSSES

1. _____

2. _____

3. _____

4. _____

5. _____

3. What do you think you would gain or hang on to, if you refused to give in to the peer pressure you face?

MY GAINS

1. _____

2. _____

3. _____

4. _____

5. _____

4. Which of these two lists is more important to you? Why?

_____

_____

_____

5. Which list consists of things that can be re-gained if lost? Explain.

_____

_____

_____

6. Comparing Joseph to Peter (last chapter), who would you say was more free? Explain.

_____

_____

_____

7. Summarize any new discoveries you have made about peer pressure from this chapter.

_____

_____

_____

Between the Lines

1. If you were to chart your willingness to pay the price for standing up to peer pressure, where would you put an "X" on the line below?

☐ ─────────────────────────────────────── ☐
Scared   **Standing**
Stiff!   **Tall!**

2. Is there one small stand you can take right now that could move your "X" a little further to the right? Will you do it?

3. Is there a friendship you need to break off because of what it is doing to you? Do it!

4. Read the story of Daniel in Daniel chapters 1–3. It is a story of courage to stand against peer pressure.

Closing Lines

One of our favorite songs is "Beat the System," sung by Petra. The first verse and the chorus radically confirm what we've looked at in this chapter:

> Caught in the undertow,
> Being swept downstream.
> Going against the flow
> Seems like such a dream.
> Trying to hold your ground,
> When you start to slide.
> Pressure to compromise
> Comes from every side.
>
> Wise up! Rise up!
> You can be more than a conqueror,
> You will never face defeat.
> You can dare to win by losing all,
> You can face the heat
> And dare to beat the system!*

*"Beat the System," by Bob Hartman. © Copyright 1985 by Dawn Treader Music. All rights reserved. Used by permission of Gaither Copyright Management.

Taking a stand, holding your ground, means high stakes. It might cost you your friends. It might determine whether or not you date on the weekends. But let us assure you of one thing—the benefits of being able to persevere against peer pressure always outweigh the price.

The ability to make choices freely, without the influence of others, is the truest evidence that you are indeed growing up instead of just growing older.

Have you been wondering whatever happened to me that lonely night? I lost my chance to get accepted into a group I greatly admired. Instead, I went home, sad and disgusted about the decision I had made. My friends? Three of them were killed instantly that night in a head-on collision as they left the bar. Who do you think paid the highest cost for the decision that night, me or them?

Lifeline:

It *costs* to resist peer pressure. But it *pays* more!

His Lines

Daniel 3:17,18

Deuteronomy 31:6

The Bottom Line (For Group Discussion)

1. Why is it so hard to resist peer pressure?

2. Do the people who put pressure on us have pressure on them? Explain your answer.

3. Why is the ability to make right choices in the face of pressure from my friends an evidence that I really know who I am?